"BE·MUCH OCCUPIED
—— WITH ——
JESUS"

SEA HARP PRESS

SEA HARP TIMELESS

Other books in the series

The Simple Way of Prayer

A Method of Union with Christ

Contents

Foreword

JEANNE-MARIE BOUVIER DE LA MOTTE-GUYON, more commonly known as Madame Guyon, was imprisoned for eight years because of the book you hold in your hands. Though an aristocrat by birth, though a widow and mother to three, though a cousin of the famous François Fénelon, such teachings of direct access to the Presence of God were intolerable to the religious authorities of her day. She ended up locked up in the Bastille. And perhaps it was because of words like these:

> If all who laboured for the conversion of others were to introduce them immediately into Prayer and the Interior Life, and make it their main design to gain and win over the heart, numberless as well as permanent conversions would certainly ensue. On the contrary, few and transient fruits must attend that labour

which is confined to outward matters; such as burdening the disciple with a thousand precepts for external exercises, instead of leaving the soul to Christ by the occupation of the heart in Him...

The decay of internal piety is unquestionably the source of the various errors that have arisen in the Church; all which would speedily be sapped and overthrown should inward religion be re-established. Errors are only so far prejudicial to the soul as they tend to weaken faith and deter from prayer; and if, instead of engaging our wandering brethren in vain disputes, we could but teach them simply to believe and diligently to pray, we should lead them sweetly unto God.

O how inexpressibly great is the loss sustained by mankind from the neglect of the Interior Life! And how tremendous must the great day of retribution be to those who are entrusted with the care of souls, for not having discovered and dispensed to their flock this hidden treasure...

Madame Guyon believed that conversion necessarily called for its next stage: a robust spiritual life of prayer and interiority. She believed that the gaining and winning of the human heart was the work of

Christ alone; that all fruitfulness with Him was found in inwardness, first, followed by external expression. She saw many of the same problems we see today in the life of the Church: the same decay, similar errors, weak faith, lack of prayer. And so, with her lovely disposition and personal experience of the living Spirit of Jesus, she endeavored to lead her readers into the wonders of the Interior Life.

Madame Guyon was willing to endure the Bastille for its sake.

May we learn from *her* for the sake of Jesus' work in us.

Thank you for being part of the Sea Harp Family!

SEA HARP
PRESS

Preface

THIS LITTLE TREATISE, conceived in great simplicity, was not originally intended for publication: it was written for a few individuals, who were desirous to love God with their whole heart; some of whom, because of the profit they received in reading the manuscript, wished to obtain copies of it; and on this account alone, it was committed to the press.

It still remains in its original simplicity, without any censure on the various Divine Leadings of others: and we submit the whole to the judgment of those who are skilled and experienced in Divine matters; requesting them, however, not to decide without first entering into the main design of the Author, which is to induce the world to love God and to serve Him with comfort and success, in a simple and easy manner, adapted to those who are unqualified for learned and deep researches, and are, indeed, incapable of anything but a hearty desire to be truly devoted to God.

An unprejudiced reader may find hidden under the most common expressions, a secret unction, which will excite him to seek after that Sovereign Good, whom all should wish to enjoy.

In speaking of the attainment of perfection, the word *facility* is used, because God is indeed found with facility when we seek Him within ourselves. But, in contradiction to this, some perhaps may urge that passage in St. John, *"Ye shall seek me, and shall not find me"* (John 7:34). This apparent difficulty, however, is removed by another passage, where He, who cannot contradict Himself, hath said to all, "*Seek and ye shall find*" (Matthew 7:7). It is true, indeed, that he who would seek God, and is yet unwilling to forsake his sins, shall not find Him, because he seeks not aright; and therefore it is added, *"Ye shall die in your sins."* On the other hand, he who diligently seeks God in his heart, and that he may draw near unto Him sincerely forsakes sin, shall infallibly find Him.

A life of devotion appears so formidable, and the Spirit of Prayer of such difficult attainment, that most persons are discouraged from taking a single step towards it. The difficulties inseparable from all great undertakings are, indeed, either nobly surmounted, or left to subsist in all their terrors, just as success is the object of despair or hope. I have therefore endeavoured to show the facility of the method proposed in this treatise, the great advantages to be derived from it, and the certainty of their attainment by those that faithfully persevere.

O were we once truly sensible of the goodness of God toward His poor creatures, and of His infinite desire to communicate Himself unto them, we should not allow imaginary difficulties to affright us, nor despair of obtaining that good which He is so earnest to bestow: *"He that spared not his own son, but delivered him up for us all; how shall he not, with him, also freely give us all things?"* (Romans 8:32). But we want courage and perseverance; we have both to a high degree in our temporal concerns, but want them in *"the one thing needful"* (Luke 10:42).

If any think that God is not easily to be found in this way of Simple Love and Pure Adherence, let them not, on my testimony, alter their opinion, but rather make trial of it, and their own experience will convince them that the reality far exceeds all my representations of it.

Beloved reader, peruse this little treatise with a humble, sincere, and candid spirit, and not with an inclination to cavil and criticize, and you will not fail to reap some degree of profit from it. It was written with a hearty desire that you might wholly devote yourself to God; receive it, then, with a like desire for your own perfection: for nothing more is intended by it than to invite the simple and childlike to approach their Father, who delights in the humble confidence of His children, and is grieved at the smallest instance of their diffidence or distrust. With a sincere desire, therefore, to forsake sin, seek nothing from the unpretending method here proposed but the love of God, and you shall undoubtedly obtain it.

Without setting up our opinions above those of others, we mean only, with truth and candour, to declare, from our own experience and the experience of others, the happy effects produced by thus simply following our Lord.

As this treatise was intended only to instruct in prayer, there are many things which we respect and esteem, totally omitted, as not immediately relative to our main subject: it is, however, certain, that nothing will be found herein to offend, provided it be read in the spirit with which it was written; and it is still more certain, that those who in right earnest make trial of the way, will find we have written the Truth.

It is Thou alone, O Holy Jesus, who lovest simplicity and innocence, *"and whose delight is to dwell with the children of men"* (Proverbs 8:31), with those who are, indeed, willing to become "little children"; it is Thou alone, who canst render this little work of any value by imprinting it on the hearts of all who read it, and leading them to seek Thee within themselves, where Thou reposest as in the manger, waiting to receive proofs of their love, and to give them testimony of Thine. Yet alas! They may still lose these unspeakable advantages by their negligence and insensibility! But it belongeth unto Thee, O thou Uncreated Love! Thou Silent and Eternal Word! it belongeth unto Thee, to awaken, attract, and convert; to make Thyself be heard, tasted, and beloved! I know Thou canst do it, and I trust Thou wilt do it by this humble work which belongeth entirely to Thee, proceedeth wholly from

Thee, and tendeth only to Thee! And, O most Gracious and adorable Saviour!

To Thee be all the glory!

Jeanne-Marie Bouvier de la Motte-Guyon
1685

I

The Universal Call to Prayer

WHAT A DREADFUL DELUSION hath prevailed over the greater part of mankind, in supposing that they are not called to a state of prayer! Whereas all are capable of prayer, and are called thereto, as all are called to and are capable of salvation.

Prayer is the application of the heart to God, and the internal exercise of love. St. Paul hath enjoined us to *"pray without ceasing"* (1 Thessalonians 5:17), and our Lord saith, *"I say unto you all, watch and pray"* (Mark 13:33, 37): all therefore may, and all ought to practice prayer. I grant that meditation is attainable but by few, for few are capable of it; and therefore, my beloved brethren who are athirst for salvation, meditative prayer is not the prayer which God requires of you, nor which we would recommend.

Let all pray: we should live by prayer, as we should live by love. *"I counsel you to buy of me gold tried in the fire, that ye may be rich"* (Revelation 3:18); this is much more easily obtained than we can conceive. *"Come, all ye that are athirst, to these living waters";* nor lose your precious moments in *"hewing out cisterns, broken cisterns that will hold no water"* (John 7:37; Jeremiah 2:13). Come, ye famished souls, who find naught whereon to feed; come, and ye shall be fully satisfied!

Come, ye poor afflicted ones, who groan beneath your load of wretchedness and pain, and ye shall find ease and comfort! Come, ye sick, to your Physician, and be not fearful of approaching Him because ye are filled with diseases; expose them to His view and they shall be healed!

Children, draw near to your Father, and He will embrace you in the arms of love! Come, ye poor, stray, wandering sheep, return to your Shepherd! Come, sinners, to your Saviour! Come, ye dull, ignorant, and illiterate, ye who think yourselves the most incapable of prayer! Ye are more peculiarly called and adapted thereto. Let all without exception come, for Jesus Christ hath called all.

Yet let not those come who are without a heart; they are not asked; for there must be a heart, that there may be love. But who is without a heart? O come, then, give this heart to God; and here learn how to make the donation.

All who are desirous of prayer may easily pray, enabled by those ordinary graces and gifts of the Holy Spirit which are common to all men.

Prayer is the guide to perfection and the sovereign good; it delivers us from every vice, and obtains for us every virtue; for the one great means to become perfect is to walk in the presence of God: He Himself hath said, *"walk in my presence and be ye perfect"* (Genesis 17:1). It is by prayer alone, that we are brought into this presence, and maintained in it without interruption.

You must then learn a species of prayer, which may be exercised at all times; which doth not obstruct outward employments; and which may be equally practiced by princes, kings, prelates, priests and magistrates, soldiers and children, tradesmen, labourers, women, and sick persons: it cannot, therefore, be the prayer of the head, but of the heart; not a prayer of the understanding alone, which is so limited in its operations that it can have but one object at one time; but the prayer of the heart is not interrupted by the exercises of reason: indeed nothing can interrupt this prayer, but irregular and disordered affections: and when once we have tasted of God, and the sweetness of His love, we shall find it impossible to relish aught but Himself.

Nothing is so easily obtained as the possession and enjoyment of God, for *"in him we live, move, and have our being"*; and He is more desirous to give Himself into us, than we can be to receive Him.

All consists in the manner of seeking Him; and to seek aright, is easier and more natural to us than breathing. Though you think yourselves ever so stupid, dull, and incapable of sublime attainments, yet, by prayer, you may live in God Himself with less difficulty or interruption than you live in the vital air. Will it not then be highly sinful to neglect prayer? But this I trust you will not, when you have learnt the method, which is exceedingly easy.

II

The Method of Prayer

THERE ARE TWO WAYS of introducing a soul into prayer, which should for some time be pursued; the one is meditation, the other is reading accompanied with meditation.

Meditative reading is the choosing of some important practical or speculative truth, always preferring the practical, and proceeding thus: whatever truth you have chosen, read only a small portion of it, endeavouring to taste and digest it, to extract the essence and substance thereof, and proceed no farther while any savour or relish remains in the passage: when this subsides, take up your book again and proceed as before, seldom reading more than half a page at a time, for it is not the quantity that is read, but the manner of reading, that yields us profit.

Those who read fast reap no more advantage than a bee would by only skimming over the surface of the flower, instead of waiting to penetrate into it, and extract its sweets. Much reading is rather for scholastic subjects than divine truths: indeed, to receive real profit from spiritual books, we must read as I have described; and I am certain, if that method were pursued, we should become gradually habituated to, and more fully disposed for prayer.

Meditation, which is the other method, is to be practiced at an appropriated season, and not in the time of reading. I believe the best manner of meditating is as follows:—When, by an act of lively faith, you are placed in the Presence of God, recollect some truth wherein there is substance and food; pause gently and sweetly thereon, not to employ the reason, but merely to calm and fix the mind: for you must observe, that your principal exercise should ever be the Presence of God; your subject, therefore, should rather serve to stay the mind, than exercise the understanding.

From this procedure, it will necessarily follow, that the lively faith in a God immediately present in our inmost soul, will produce an eager and vehement pressing inwardly into ourselves, and a restraining of all our senses from wandering abroad: this serves to extricate us speedily from numberless distractions, to remove us far from external objects, and to bring us nigh unto our God, Who is only to be found in our inmost centre, which is the Holy of Holies wherein He dwelleth.

He hath even promised *"to come and make his abode with him that doth his will"* (John 14:23). St. Augustine accuses himself of wasting his time, by not having from the first sought God in this manner of prayer.

When we are thus fully introverted, and warmly penetrated throughout with a living sense of the Divine Presence; when the senses are all recollected, and withdrawn from the circumference to the centre, and the soul is sweetly and silently employed on the truths we have read, not in reasoning, but in feeding thereon, and in animating the will by affection, rather than fatiguing the understanding by study; when, I say, the affections are in this state, which, however difficult it may appear at first, is, as I shall hereafter show, easily attainable; we must allow them sweetly to repose, and peacefully to drink in that of which they have tasted: for as a person may enjoy the flavour of the finest viand in mastication, yet receive no nourishment therefrom, if he does not cease the action and swallow the food; so, when our affections are enkindled, if we endeavour to stir them up yet more, we extinguish their flame, and the soul is deprived of its nourishment; we should, therefore, in stillness and repose, with respect, confidence, and love, swallow the blessed food of which we have tasted: this method is, indeed, highly necessary, and will advance the soul farther in a short time, than any other in a course of years.

I have mentioned that our direct and principal exercise should consist in the contemplation of the Divine Presence: we should be also exceedingly watchful and diligent in recalling our dissipated senses, as the most easy method of overcoming distractions; for a direct contest and opposition only serves to irritate and augment them; whereas, by sinking down under a sense and perception of a present God, and by simply turning inwards, we wage insensibly a very advantageous, though indirect war with them.

It is proper here to caution beginners against wandering from truth to truth, and from subject to subject: the right way to penetrate every divine truth, to enjoy its full relish, and to imprint it on the heart, is dwelling on it whilst its savour continues.

Though recollection is difficult in the beginning, from the habit the soul has acquired of being always from home; yet, when by the violence it hath done itself, it becometh a little accustomed to it, it will soon be rendered perfectly easy, and become delightful. Such is the experimental taste and sense of His Presence, and such the efficacy of those graces, which that God bestows, Whose One Will towards His creatures is to communicate Himself unto them!

III

The First Degree of Prayer

THOSE WHO HAVE NOT LEARNT to read, are not, on that account, excluded from prayer; for the Great Book which teacheth all things, and which is legible as well internally as externally, is Jesus Christ Himself.

The method they should practice is this: They should first learn this fundamental truth, that *"the kingdom of God is within them"* (Luke 17:21), and that it is there, only it must be sought.

It is as incumbent on the clergy, to instruct their parishioners in prayer, as in their catechism. It is true, they tell them the end of their creation; but should they not also give them sufficient instructions how they may attain it? They should be taught to begin by an act of profound adoration and abasement before God; and closing the corporeal eyes, endeavour to open those of the soul: they should then collect themselves inwardly, and, by a lively faith in God, as dwelling within them, pierce into the Divine Presence;

not suffering the senses to wander abroad, but withholding them as much as may be in due subjection.

They should then repeat the Lord's Prayer in their native tongue, pondering a little upon the meaning of the words, and the infinite willingness of that God Who dwells within them, to become, indeed, their Father. In this state let them pour out their wants before Him; and when they have pronounced the endearing word, Father, remain a few moments in a respectful silence, waiting to have the will of this their heavenly Father made manifest unto them.

Again, beholding themselves in the state of a feeble child, sorely bruised by repeated falls, and defiled in the mire, destitute of strength to keep up, or of power to cleanse himself, they should lay their deplorable situation open to their Father's view in humble confusion; now sighing out a few words of love and plaintive sorrow, and again sinking into profound silence before Him. Then, continuing the Lord's Prayer, let them beseech this King of Glory to reign in them, yielding to His love the just claim He has over them, and resigning up themselves wholly to His divine government.

If they feel an inclination to peace and silence, let them discontinue the words of the prayer so long as this sensation holds;

and when it subsides, go on with the second petition, "*Thy will be done on earth, as it is in heaven!*" upon which these humble supplicants must beseech God to accomplish, in them, and by them, all His will; and must surrender their hearts and freedom into His hands, to be disposed of as He pleaseth. And finding that the best employment of the will is to love, they should desire to love God with all their strength, and implore Him for His pure love; but all this sweetly and peacefully: and so of the rest of the prayer, in which the clergy may instruct them. But they should not overburden themselves with frequent repetitions of set forms or studied prayers (Matthew 6:7); for the Lord's Prayer, once repeated as I have just described, will produce abundant fruit.

At other times they should place themselves as sheep before their Shepherd, looking up to Him for their true substantial food: "*O Divine Shepherd, Thou feedest Thy flock with Thyself, and art, indeed, their daily nourishment!*" They may also represent unto Him the necessities of their families: but all upon this principle, and in this one great view of faith, that God is within them.

The ideas we form of the Divine Being fall infinitely short of what He is: a lively faith in His presence is sufficient: for we must not form any image of the Deity; though we may of the Second Person in the ever-blessed Trinity, beholding Him in the various states of His incarnation, from His birth to His crucifixion, or in some other state or mystery, provided the soul always seeks for those views in its inmost ground or centre.

Again, we may look to Him as our Physician, and present to His healing influence all our maladies; but always without violence or perturbation, and from time to time with pauses of silence, that being intermingled with the action, the silence may be gradually extended, and our own exertion lessened; till at length, by continually yielding to God's operations, they gain the complete ascendancy; as shall be hereafter explained.

When the Divine Presence is granted to us, and we gradually relish silence and repose, this experimental feeling and taste of the Presence of God introduces the soul into the second degree of prayer, which, by proceeding in the manner I have described, is attainable as well by the illiterate as the learned: some favoured souls, indeed, are indulged with it, even from the beginning.

IV

The Second Degree of Prayer

SOME CALL THE SECOND DEGREE of prayer, "The Prayer of Contemplation," "The Prayer of Faith and Stillness," and others call it, "The Prayer of Simplicity." I shall here use this latter appellation, as being more just than any of the former, which imply a much more exalted state of prayer than that I am now treating of.

When the soul has been for some time exercised in the way I have mentioned, it finds that it is gradually enabled to approach God with facility; that recollection is attended with much less difficulty; and that prayer becomes easy, sweet, and delightful; it knows that this is the true way of finding God; and feels "*his name is as ointment poured forth*" (Canticles 1-3). But the method must now be altered, and that which I prescribe, followed with courage and fidelity, without being disturbed at the difficulties we may encounter therein.

First, as soon as the soul by faith places itself in the Presence of God, and becomes recollected before Him, let it remain thus for a little time in a profound and respectful silence.

But if, at the beginning, in forming the act of faith, it feels some little pleasing sense of the Divine Presence; let it remain there without being troubled for a subject, and proceed no farther, but carefully cherish this sensation while it continues: as soon as it abates, the will may be excited by some tender affection; and if by the first moving thereof, it finds itself reinstated in sweet peace, let it there remain: the smothered fire must be gently fanned; but as soon as it is kindled, we must cease that effort, lest we extinguish it by our own activity.

I would warmly recommend it to all, never to finish prayer, without remaining some little time after in a respectful silence. It is also of the greatest importance for the soul to go to prayer with courage, and such a pure and disinterested love, as seeks nothing from God, but the ability to please Him, and to do His will: for a servant who only proportions his diligence to his hope of reward, renders himself unworthy of all reward.

Go then to prayer, not that ye may enjoy spiritual delights, but that ye may be either full or empty, just as it pleaseth God: this will

preserve you in an evenness of spirit, in deser-
tion as well as in consolation, and prevent
your being surprised at aridity or the apparent
repulses of God.

V

Of Spiritual Aridity

THOUGH GOD HATH NO OTHER DESIRE than to impart Himself to the loving soul that seeks Him, yet He frequently conceals Himself that the soul may be roused from sloth, and impelled to seek Him with fidelity and love. But with what abundant goodness doth He recompense the faithfulness of His beloved? And how sweetly are these apparent withdrawings of Himself succeeded by the consoling caresses of love?

At these seasons we are apt to believe, either that it proves our fidelity, and evinces a greater ardour of affection, to seek Him by an exertion of our own strength and activity; or, that this exertion will induce Him the more speedily to revisit us. No, no, my dear souls, believe me, this is not the right procedure in this degree of prayer; with patient love, with self-abasement and humiliation, with the reiterated breathings of an ardent but peaceful affection, and with silence full of the most profound respect, you must wait the return of the Beloved. Thus only you will demonstrate that it is Himself alone, and His good pleasure, that you seek; and not the selfish delights of your own sensations. Hence it is said, "*Be not impatient in the time of dryness and obscurity; suffer the suspension and delays of the consolations of God; cleave unto him, and wait upon him, patiently, that thy life may increase and be renewed*" (Ecclesiastes 2:2-3).

Be ye, therefore, patient in prayer, though, during life, you can do naught else than wait the return of the Beloved, in deep humiliation, calm contentment, and patient resignation to His will. And yet how this most excellent prayer may be intermingled with the sighings of plaintive love! This conduct, indeed, is most pleasing to the heart of Jesus; and, above all others, will, as it were, compel Him to return.

VI

Of Self-Surrender

WE SHOULD NOW BEGIN to abandon and give up our whole existence unto God, from the strong and positive conviction, that the occurrence of every moment is agreeable to His immediate will and permission, and just such as our state requires. This conviction will make us resigned in all things; and accept of all that happens, not as from the creature, but as from God Himself.

But I conjure you, my dearly beloved, who sincerely wish to give up yourselves to God, that after you have made the donation, you will not snatch yourselves back again: remember, a gift once presented, is no longer at the disposal of the donor.

Abandonment is a matter of the greatest importance in our process; it is the key to the inner court; so that whosoever knoweth truly how to abandon himself, soon becomes perfect: we must, therefore, continue steadfast and immovable therein, nor listen to the voice of natural reason. Great faith produces great abandonment: we must confide in God *"hoping against hope"* (Romans 4:18).

Abandonment is the casting off of all selfish care, that we may be altogether at the Divine disposal. All Christians are exhorted to this resignation: for it is said to all, *"Be not anxious for tomorrow, for your Heavenly Father knoweth all that is necessary for you"* (Matthew 20:25). *"In all thy ways acknowledge him, and he shall direct thy paths"* (Proverbs 3:6). *"Commit thy ways unto the Lord, and thy thoughts shall be established"* (Proverbs 16:3). *"Commit thy ways unto the Lord, and he himself will bring it to pass"* (Psalm 36:5).

Our abandonment then should be as fully applied to external as internal things, giving up all our concerns into the hands of God, forgetting ourselves, and thinking only of Him; by which the heart will remain always disengaged, free, and at peace. It is practiced by continually losing our own will in the will of God; by renouncing every particular inclination as soon as it arises, however good it may appear, that we may stand in indifference with respect to ourselves, and only will that which God from eternity hath willed; by being resigned in all things, whether for soul or body, whether for time or eternity; by leaving what is past in oblivion, what is to come to Providence, and devoting the present moment to God, which brings with itself God's eternal order, and is as infallible a declaration to us of His will as it is inevitable and common to all; by attributing nothing that befalls us to the creature, but regarding all things in God, and looking upon all, excepting only our sins, as infallibly proceeding from Him. Surrender yourselves, then, to be led and disposed of just as God pleaseth, with respect both to your outward and inward state.

VII

Of Sufferings

BE PATIENT UNDER ALL THE SUFFERINGS which God is pleased to send you: if your love to Him be pure, you will not seek Him less on Calvary, than on Tabor; and, surely, He should be as much loved on that as on this, since it was on Calvary He made the greater display of His love for you.

Be not like those, who give themselves to Him at one season, and withdraw from Him at another: they give themselves only to be caressed; and wrest themselves back again, when they come to be crucified, or at least turn for consolation to the creature.

No, beloved souls, ye will not find consolation in aught, but in the love of the Cross, and in total abandonment: *"Whosoever favoureth not the Cross, favoureth not the things that be of God"* (Matthew 16:23). It is impossible to love God without loving the Cross; and a heart that favours the Cross, finds the bitterest things to be sweet: *"A famished soul findeth bitter things sweet"* (Job 6:1) because it findeth itself hungering for God, in proportion as it hungereth for the Cross. God giveth the Cross, and the Cross giveth us God.

We may be assured, that there is an internal advancement, where there is an advancement in the way of the Cross: Abandonment and the Cross go hand in hand together.

As soon as suffering presents itself, and you feel a repugnance against it, resign yourself immediately unto God with respect to it, and give yourself up to Him in sacrifice; you shall find, that, when the Cross arrives, it will not be so very burdensome, because you had disposed yourself to a willing reception of it. This, however, does not prevent your feeling its weight as some have imagined; for when we do not feel the Cross, we do not suffer it. A sensibility of sufferings constitutes a principal part of the sufferings themselves. Jesus Christ Himself was willing to suffer its utmost rigours. We often bear the Cross in weakness, at other times in strength; all should be equal to us in the will of God.

Of Mysteries

IT MAY BE OBJECTED, that, by this method, we shall have no mysteries imprinted on our minds: but it is quite the reverse; for it is the peculiar means of imparting them to the soul. Jesus Christ, to whom we are abandoned, and whom *"we follow as the way, whom we hear as the truth, and who animates us as the life"* (John 14:6) in imprinting Himself on the soul, impresses the characters of His different states; and to bear all the states of Jesus Christ is far more sublime, than merely to reason concerning them. St. Paul bore in his body the states of Jesus Christ: *"I bear in my body,"* says he, *"the marks of the Lord Jesus"* (Galatians 6:17), but he does not say that he reasoned thereon.

In our acts of resignation, Jesus Christ frequently communicates some peculiar views or revelations of His states: these we should thankfully receive, and dispose ourselves for what appeareth to be His will. Indeed, having no other choice, but that of ardently reaching after Him, of dwelling ever with Him, and of sinking into nothingness before Him, we should accept indiscriminately all His dispensations, whether obscurity or illumination, fruitfulness or barrenness, weakness or strength, sweetness or bitterness, temptations, distractions, pain, weariness, or doubtings; and none of all these should, for one moment, retard our course.

God engages some, for whole years, in the contemplation and enjoyment of a particular mystery; the simple view or contemplation of which gathers the soul inward, provided it be faithful: but as soon as God is pleased to withdraw this view from the soul, it should freely yield to the deprivation. Some are very uneasy at feeling their inability to meditate on certain mysteries; but this disquietude hath no just foundation, since an affectionate attachment to God includes every species of devotion: for whosoever, in repose and quiet, is united to God alone, is, indeed, most excellently and effectually applied to every divine mystery: the love of God comprehends, in itself, the love of all that appertains to Him.

Of Virtue

IT IS THUS WE ACQUIRE virtue, with facility and cer-tainty; for, as God is the fountain and principle of all virtue, we possess all in the possession of Himself; and in proportion as we approach towards this possession, in like proportion do we rise into the most eminent virtues. For all virtue is but as a mask, an outside appearance changeable as our garments, if it doth not spring up, and issue from within; and then, indeed, it is genuine, essential, and permanent: *"The beauty of the King's daughter proceeds from within,"* saith David (Psalm 45:14). These souls, above all others, practice virtue in the most eminent degree, though they advert not to virtue in particular; God, to whom they are united, carries them to the most extensive practice of it; He is exceedingly jealous over them, and prohibits them the taste of any pleasure but in Himself.

What a hungering for sufferings have those souls, who thus glow with Divine love! How prone to precipitate into excessive austerities, were they permitted to pursue their own inclinations! They think of nought save how they may please their Beloved: as their self-love abates, they neglect and forget themselves; and as their love to God increases, so do self-detestation and disregard to the creature.

O was this easy method acquired, a method so suited to all, to the dull and ignorant as well as to the acute and learned, how easily would the whole Church of God be reformed! Love only is required: "Love," saith St. Augustine, "and then do what you please." For when we truly love, we cannot have so much as a will to anything that might offend the Object of our affections.

X

Of Mortification

I WILL EVEN AFFIRM, that, in any other way, it is next to an impossibility ever to acquire a perfect mortification of the senses and passions.

The reason is obvious; the soul gives vigour and energy to the senses, and the senses raise and stimulate the passions: a dead body has neither sensations nor passions, because its connection with the soul is dissolved.

All endeavours merely to rectify the exterior, impel the soul yet farther outward into that about which it is so warmly and zealously engaged. It is in these matters that its powers are diffused and scattered abroad: for its application being immediately directed to austerities, and other externals, it thus invigorates those very senses it is aiming to subdue. For the senses have no other spring from whence to derive their vigour, than the application of the soul to themselves; the degree of their life and activity is proportioned to the degree of attention which the soul bestows upon them; and this life of the senses stirs up and provokes the passions, instead of suppressing or subduing them: austerities may, indeed, enfeeble the body, but, for the reasons just mentioned, can never take off the keenness of the senses, or lessen their activity.

The only method to effect this is inward recollection; by which the soul is turned wholly and altogether inward, to possess a present God. If the soul directs all its vigour and energy towards this centre of its being, the simple act separates and withdraws it from the senses; the exercising of all its powers internally leaves them faint and impotent; and the nearer it draws to God, the farther is it separated from the senses, and the less are the passions influenced by them.

Hence it is, that those, in whom the attractions of grace are very powerful, find the outward man altogether weak and feeble, and even liable to faintings. I do not mean by this to discourage mortification; for it should ever accompany prayer, according to the strength and state of the person, or as obedience will allow. But I say that mortification should not be our principal exercise; nor should we prescribe ourselves such and such austerities, but follow simply and merely the internal attractions of grace; and being possessed and occupied with the Divine Presence (without thinking particularly on mortification) God will enable us to perform every species of it; and most assuredly He will give no relaxation to those who abide faithful in their abandonment to Him, until He has mortified in them everything that remains to be mortified.

We have only then to continue steadfast in the utmost attention to God, and all things will be rightly performed. All are not capable of outward austerities, but all are capable of this. In the mortification of the eye and ear, which continually supply the busy imagination with new objects, there is little danger of falling into excess: but God will teach us this also, and we have only to follow where His Spirit guides.

The soul has a double advantage by proceeding thus, for, in withdrawing from outward objects, it draws the nearer to God; and in approaching Him, besides the secret sustaining and preserving power and virtue received, it is the farther removed from sin, the nearer the approach is made; so that conversion becomes habitual.

XI

Of Conversion

"*BE YE TRULY CONVERTED unto that God from whom ye have so deeply revolted*" (Isaiah 31:6). To be truly converted is to avert wholly from the creature, and turn wholly unto God.

For the attainment of salvation it is absolutely necessary that we should forsake outward sin and turn unto righteousness: but this alone is not perfect conversion, which consists in a total change of the whole man from an outward to an inward life.

When the soul is once turned to God a wonderful facility is found in continuing steadfast in conversion; and the longer it remains thus converted, the nearer it approaches, and the more firmly it adheres to God; and the nearer it draws to Him, of necessity it is the farther removed from the creature, which is so contrary to Him: so that it is so effectually established and rooted in its conversion that it becomes habitual, and, as it were, natural.

Now we must not suppose that this is effected by a violent exertion of its own powers; for it is not capable of, nor should it attempt any other cooperation with Divine Grace, than that of endeavouring to withdraw itself from external objects and to turn inwards: after which it has nothing farther to do than to continue steadfast in adherence to God.

God has an attractive virtue which draws the soul more and more powerfully to Himself, the nearer it approaches towards Him, and, in attracting, He purifies and refines it; just as with a gross vapour exhaled by the sun, which, as it gradually ascends, is rarified and rendered pure, the vapour, indeed, contributes to its exhalation only by its passiveness; but the soul cooperates with the attractions of God, by a free and affectionate correspondence. This kind of introversion is both easy and efficacious, advancing the soul naturally and without constraint, because God Himself is its centre.

Every centre has a powerfully attractive virtue; and the more pure and exalted it is, the stronger and more irresistible are its attractions. But besides the potent magnetism of the centre itself, there is, in every creature, a correspondent tendency to re-union with its peculiar centre which is vigorous and active in proportion to the spirituality and perfection of the subject.

As soon as anything is turned towards its centre its own gravitation instigates and accelerates it thereto, unless it be withheld by some invincible obstacle: a stone held in the hand is no sooner disengaged than by its own weight it falls to the earth as to its centre; so also water and fire, when unobstructed, tend and flow incessantly to their principle or centre. Now, when the soul, by its efforts to abandon outward objects, and gather itself inwards, is brought into the influence of this central tendency, without any other exertion, it falls gradually by the weight of Divine Love into its proper centre; and the more passive and tranquil it remains, and the freer from self-motion and self-exertion, the more rapidly it advances, because the energy of the central attractive virtue is unobstructed and has full liberty for action.

All our care and attention should, therefore, be to acquire inward recollection: nor let us be discouraged by the pains and difficulties we encounter in this exercise, which will soon be recompensed, on the part of our God, by such abundant supplies of grace as will render the exercise perfectly easy, provided we be faithful in meekly withdrawing our hearts from outward distractions and occupations, and returning to our centre with affections full of tenderness and serenity. When at any time the passions are turbulent, a gentle retreat inwards unto a Present God, easily deadens and pacifies them; and any other way of contending with them rather irritates than appeases them.

Of the Presence of God

THE SOUL THAT IS FAITHFUL in the exercise of love and adherence to God above described, is astonished to feel Him gradually taking possession of their whole being: it now enjoys a continual sense of that Presence, which is become as it were natural to it; and this, as well as prayer, is the result of habit. The soul feels an unusual serenity gradually being diffused throughout all its faculties; and silence now wholly constitutes its prayer; whilst God communicates an intuitive love, which is the beginning of ineffable blessedness. O that I were permitted to pursue this subject and describe some degrees of the endless progression of subsequent states! But I now write only for beginners; and shall, therefore, proceed no farther, but wait our Lord's time for publishing what may be applicable to every conceivable degree of "stature in Christ Jesus."

We must, however, urge it as a matter of the highest import, to cease from self-action and self-exertion, that

God Himself may act alone: He saith, by the mouth of His Prophet David, "*Be still, and know that I am God*" (Psalm 46:10). But the creature is so infatuated with a love and attachment to its own workings, that it imagines nothing at all is done, if it doth not perceive and distinguish all its operations. It is ignorant that its inability minutely to observe the manner of its motion is occasioned by the swiftness of its progress; and that the operations of God, in extending and diffusing their influence, absorb those of the creature. The stars may be seen distinctly before the sun rises; but as his light advances, their rays are gradually absorbed by his and they become invisible, not from the want of light in themselves, but from the superior effulgence of the chief luminary.

The case is similar here; for there is a strong and universal light which absorbs all the little distinct lights of the soul; they grow faint and disappear under its powerful influence, and self-activity is now no longer distinguishable: yet those greatly err who accuse this prayer of idleness, a charge that can arise only from inexperience. If they would but make some efforts towards the attainment of this prayer, they would soon experience the contrary of what they suppose and find their accusation groundless.

This appearance of inaction is, indeed, not the consequence of sterility and want, but of fruitfulness and abundance which will be clearly perceived by the experienced soul, who will know and feel that the silence is full and unctuous, and the result of causes totally the reverse of apathy and barrenness. There are two kinds of people that keep silence; the one because they have nothing to say, the other because they have too much: it is so with the soul in this state; the silence is occasioned by the superabundance of matter, too great for utterance.

To be drowned, and to die of thirst, are deaths widely different; yet water may, in some sense, be said to cause both; abundance destroys in one case, and want in the other. So in this state the abundance and overflowings of grace still the activity of self; and, therefore, it is of the utmost importance to remain as silent as possible.

The infant hanging at the mother's breast is a lively illustration of our subject: it begins to draw the milk by moving its little lips; but when the milk flows abundantly, it is content to swallow, and suspends its suction: by doing otherwise it would only hurt itself, spill the milk, and be obliged to quit the breast.

We must act in like manner in the beginning of Prayer, by exerting the lips of the affections;

but as soon as the milk of Divine Grace flows freely, we have nothing to do but, in repose and stillness, sweetly to imbibe it; and when it ceases to flow, we must again stir up the affections as the infant moves its lips. Whoever acts otherwise cannot turn this grace to advantage, which is bestowed to allure and draw the soul into the repose of love, and not into the multiplicity of self.

But what becometh of this child, who gently and without motion drinketh in the milk? Who would believe that it can thus receive nourishment? Yet the more peacefully it feeds, the better it thrives. What, I say, becomes of this infant? It drops gently asleep on its mother's bosom. So the soul that is tranquil and peaceful in prayer, sinketh frequently into a mystic slumber, wherein all its powers are at rest; till at length it is wholly fitted for that state, of which it enjoys these transient anticipations. In this process the soul is led naturally, without effort, art, or study.

The Interior is not a stronghold to be taken by storm and violence, but a kingdom of peace, which is to be gained only by love.

If any will thus pursue the little path I have pointed out, it will lead them to intuitive prayer. God demands nothing extraordinary nor difficult; on the contrary, He is best pleased by a simple and child-like conduct.

That which is most sublime and elevated in religion is the easiest attained: the most necessary sacraments are the least difficult. It is thus also in natural things: if you would go to sea, embark on a river, and you will be conveyed to it insensibly and without exertion. Would you go to God, follow this sweet and simple path, and you will arrive at the desired object, with an ease and expedition that will amaze you.

O that you would but once make the trial! How soon would you find that all I have advanced falls short of the reality, and that your own experience will carry you infinitely beyond it! Is it fear that prevents you from instantly casting yourself into those arms of love, which were widely extended on the cross only to receive you? Whence can your fears arise? What risk do you run, in depending solely on your God, and abandoning yourself wholly unto Him? Ah! He will not deceive you, unless by bestowing an abundance beyond your highest hopes: but those who expect all from themselves will inevitably be deceived, and must suffer this rebuke of God by His prophet Isaiah, "*Ye have wearied yourselves in the multiplicity of your ways, and have not said let us rest in peace*" (Isaiah 57:10, Vulgate).

XIII

Of Rest before God

THE SOUL ADVANCED THUS FAR hath no need of any other preparation than its quietude: for now the Presence of God, which is the great effect, or rather continuation of Prayer, begins to be infused, and almost without intermission. The soul enjoys transcendent blessedness, and feels that "it no longer lives, but that Christ liveth in it"; and that the only way to find Him is introversion. No sooner do the bodily eyes close than the soul is wrapt up in Prayer: it is amazed at so great a blessing, and enjoys an internal converse, which external matters cannot interrupt.

The same may be said of this species of prayer that is said of wisdom, *"all good things come together with her"* (Wisdom 7:11). For the virtues flow from this soul into exertion with so much sweetness and facility that they appear natural and spontaneous; and the living spring within breaks forth so freely and abundantly into all goodness that it becomes even insensible to evil. Let it then remain faithful in this state; and beware of choosing or seeking any other disposition whatsoever than this simple rest as a preparative either to confession or communion, to action or prayer, for its sole business is to expand itself for the full reception of the Divine infusions. I would not be understood to speak of the preparations necessary for the sacraments, but of the most perfect dispositions in which they can be received.

XIV

Of Inward Silence

"*THE LORD IS IN HIS HOLY TEMPLE, let all the earth keep silence before him*" (Habakkuk 2:20). Inward silence is absolutely indispensable, because the Word is essential and eternal, and necessarily requires dispositions in the soul in some degree correspondent to His nature, as a capacity for the reception of Himself. Hearing is a sense formed to receive sounds, and is rather passive than active, admitting, but not communicating sensation; and if we would hear, we must lend the ear for that purpose: so Christ, the eternal Word, without whose Divine inspeaking the soul is dead, dark, and barren, when He would speak within us, requires the most silent attention to His all-quickening and efficacious voice.

Hence it is so frequently enjoined us in Sacred Writ, to hear and be attentive to the Voice of God: of the numerous exhortations to this effect I shall quote a few: "*Hearken unto me, my people, and give ear unto me,*

O my nation!" (Isaiah 51:4), and again, "*Hear me, all ye whom I carry in my bosom, and bear within my bowels*" (Isaiah 46:3), and farther by the Psalmist "*Hearken, O daughter, and consider, and incline thine ear; forget also thine own people, and thy father's house; so shall the King greatly desire thy beauty*" (Psalm 45:10-11).

We should forget ourselves, and all self-interest, and listen and be attentive to the voice of our God: and these two simple actions, or rather passive dispositions, attract His love to that beauty which He Himself communicates.

Outward silence is very requisite for the cultivation and improvement of inward; and indeed it is impossible we should become truly internal without the love and practice of outward silence and retirement. God saith, by the mouth of His prophet, "*I will lead her into solitude, and there will I speak to her heart*" (Hosea 2:14, Vulgate); and unquestionably the being internally occupied and engaged with God is wholly incompatible with being busied and employed in the numerous trifles that surround us.

When through imbecility or unfaithfulness we become dissipated, or as it were uncentred, it is of immediate importance to turn again gently and sweetly inward; and thus we may learn to preserve the spirit and unction of prayer throughout the day; for if prayer and recollection were wholly confined to any appointed half-hour or hour, we should reap but little fruit.

XV

Of Confession
and Self-Examination

SELF-EXAMINATION SHOULD ALWAYS precede confession, and in the nature and manner of it should be conformable to the state of the soul: the business of those that are advanced to the degree of which we now treat, is to lay their whole souls open before God, who will not fail to enlighten them, and enable them to see the peculiar nature of their faults. This examination, however, should be peaceful and tranquil, and we should depend on God for the discovery and knowledge of our sins, rather than, on the diligence of our own scrutiny.

When we examine with constraint, and in the strength of our own endeavours, we are easily deceived and betrayed by self-love into error; "*we believe the evil good, and the good evil*" (Isaiah 5:20); but when we lie in full exposure before the Sun of Righteousness, His Divine beams render the smallest atoms visible. It follows from hence that we must forsake self, and abandon our souls to God as well in examination as confession.

When souls have attained to this species of prayer, no fault escapes reprehension; on every commission they are instantly rebuked by an inward burning and tender confusion. Such is the scrutiny of Him who suffers no evil to be concealed; and under His purifying influence the one way is to turn affectionately to our Judge, and bear with meekness the pain and correction He inflicts. He becomes the incessant Examiner of the soul; it can now, indeed, no longer examine itself, and if it be faithful in its resignation, experience will convince the soul that it is a thousand times more effectually examined by His Divine Light than by the most active and vigorous self-inspection.

Those who tread these paths should be informed of a matter respecting their confession in which they are apt to err. When they begin to give an account of their sins, instead of the regret and contrition they had been accustomed to feel, they find that love and tranquility sweetly pervade and take possession of their souls: now those who are not properly instructed are desirous of withdrawing from this sensation, to form an act of contrition, because they have heard, and with truth, that it is requisite: but they are not aware that they lose thereby the genuine contrition, which is this intuitive love, infinitely surpassing any effect produced by self-exertion, and comprehending the other acts in itself as in one principal act, in much higher perfection than if they were distinctly perceived, and varied in their sensation. Be not then troubled about other things when God acts so excellently in you and for you.

To hate sin in this manner is to hate it as God does. The purest love is that which is of His immediate operation in the soul: why should it then be so eager for action? Let it remain in the state He assigns it, agreeable to the instructions of Solomon: *"Put your confidence in God; remain in quiet, where he hath placed you."*

The soul will also be amazed at finding a difficulty in calling faults to remembrance: this, however, should cause no uneasiness; first, because this forgetfulness of our faults is some proof of our purification from them; and in this degree of advancement it is best. Secondly, because when confession is our duty God will not fail to make known to us our greatest faults, for then He Himself examines, and the soul will feel the end of examination more perfectly accomplished than it could possibly have been by the utmost exertion of its own endeavours.

These instructions, however, would be altogether unsuitable to the preceding degrees while the soul continues in its active state, wherein it is right and necessary it should in all things use the utmost industry in proportion to the degree of its advancement. It is those that have arrived at this more advanced state whom I would exhort to follow these instructions, and not to vary their one simple occupation even on approaching the Communion; they should remain in silence, and suffer God to act freely and without limitation. Who can better receive the Body and Blood of Christ than he in whom the Holy Spirit is indwelling?

XVI

Of Reading and Vocal Prayer

IF, WHILE READING, you feel yourself recollected, lay aside the book and remain in stillness; at all times read but little, and cease to read when you are thus internally attracted.

The soul that is called to a state of inward silence should not encumber itself with long vocal prayers; whenever it does pray vocally, and finds a difficulty therein, and an attraction to silence, it should not use constraint by persevering, but yield to the internal drawings, unless the repeating such prayers be a matter of obedience. In any other case, it is much better not to be burdened with and tied down to the repetition of set forms, but wholly given up to the leadings of the Holy Spirit; and herein, indeed, is every species of devotion inclusively fulfilled in a most eminent degree.

XVII

Of Petitions

THE SOUL SHOULD NOT BE SURPRISED at feeling itself unable to offer up to God such petitions as it had formerly made with freedom and facility; for now the Spirit maketh intercession for it according to the will of God, that *"Spirit which helpeth our infirmities: for we know not what we should pray for as we ought; but the Spirit itself maketh intercession for us, with groanings which cannot be uttered"* (Romans 8:26). We must cooperate with, and second the designs of God, which tend to divest us of all our own operations, that in the place thereof His own may be substituted. Let this then be done in you, and suffer not yourself to be attached to anything, however good it may appear; for it is no longer good if it in any measure turns you aside from that which God willeth of you: the Divine will is preferable to all things else. Shake off then all attachments to the interests of self, and live on faith and resignation; here it is that genuine faith begins truly to operate.

XVIII

Of Defects or Infirmities

SHOULD WE EITHER WANDER among externals, or sink into dissipation, or commit a fault, we must instantly turn inwards; for having departed thereby from our God, we should as soon as possible return again unto Him, and suffer in His presence whatever sensations He is pleased to impress. On the commission of a fault it is of great importance to guard against vexation and disquietude, which springs from a secret root of pride and a love of our own excellence; we are hurt by feeling what we are; and if we discourage ourselves or despond, we are the more enfeebled; and from our reflections on the fault a chagrin arises, which is often worse than the fault itself.

The truly humble soul is not surprised at defects or failings; and the more miserable and wretched it beholds itself, the more doth it abandon itself unto God, and press for a nearer and more intimate alliance with Him, that it may avail itself of His eternal strength. We should the rather be induced to act thus, as God Himself hath said, "*I will make thee understand what thou oughtest to do; I will teach thee the way by which thou shouldst go; and I will have mine eye continually upon thee for a guide*" (Psalm 32:8, Vulgate).

XIX

Of Distractions and Temptations

A DIRECT CONTEST AND STRUGGLE with distractions and temptations rather serves to augment them, and withdraws the soul from that adherence to God, which should ever be its principal occupation. The surest and safest method for conquest is simply to turn away from the evil and draw yet nearer and closer to our God. A little child, on perceiving a monster, does not wait to fight with it, and will scarcely turn its eyes towards it, but quickly shrinks into the bosom of its mother, in total confidence of safety; so likewise should the soul turn from the dangers of temptation to God. *"God is in the midst of her,"* saith the Psalmist, *"she shall not be moved; God shall help her, and that right early"* (Psalm 46:5).

If we do otherwise, and in our weakness attempt to attack our enemies, we shall frequently feel ourselves wounded, if not totally defeated; but, by casting ourselves into the simple Presence of God, we shall find instant supplies of strength for our support. This was the succor sought for by David: "*I have set,*" saith he, "*the Lord always before me: because he is at my right hand, I shall not be moved. Therefore my heart is glad, and my glory rejoiceth: my flesh also shall rest in hope*" (Psalm 16:8-9). And it is said in Exodus, "*The Lord shall fight for you, and ye shall hold your peace.*"

XX

Of Self-Annihilation

SUPPLICATION AND SACRIFICE are comprehended in prayer, which, according to St. John, is "*an incense, the smoke whereof ascendeth unto God;*" therefore it is said in the Apocalypse that "*unto the Angel was given much incense, that he should offer it with the prayers of all Saints*" (Revelation 8:3).

Prayer is the effusion of the heart in the Presence of God: "*I have poured out my soul before God*" saith the mother of Samuel (1 Samuel 1:15). The prayer of the wise men at the feet of Christ in the stable of Bethlehem, was signified by the incense they offered: for prayer being the energy and fire of love, melting, dissolving, and sublimating the soul, and causing it to ascend unto God; therefore, in proportion as the soul is melted and dissolved, in like proportion do odours issue from it; and these odours proceed from the intense fire of love within.

This is illustrated in the Canticles (Song of Songs 1:11) where the spouse saith, "*While the King sitteth on his couch, my spikenard sendeth forth the smell thereof.*" The couch is the ground or centre of the soul; and when God is there, and we know how to dwell with Him, and abide in His Presence, the sacred power and influence thereof gradually dissolves the obduration of the soul, and, as it melteth, odours issue forth: hence it is, that the Beloved saith of His spouse, in seeing her soul melt when He spake, "*Who is this that cometh out of the wilderness, like pillars of smoke perfumed with myrrh and frankincense?*" (Song of Songs 5:6 and 3:6).

Thus doth the soul ascend unto God, by giving up self to the destroying and annihilating power of Divine Love: this, indeed, is a most essential and necessary sacrifice in the Christian religion, and that alone by which we pay true homage to the sovereignty of God; as it is written, "*The power of the Lord is great, and he is honoured only by the humble*" (Ecclesiastes 3:20). By the destruction of the existence of self within us, we truly acknowledge the supreme existence of our God; for unless we cease to exist in self, the Spirit of the Eternal Word cannot exist in us: now it is by the giving up of our own life, that we give place for His coming; and "in dying to ourselves, He liveth and abideth in us."

We should, indeed, surrender our whole being unto Christ Jesus: and cease to live any longer in ourselves, that He may become our life; *"that being dead, our life may be hid with Christ in God"* (Colossians 3:3). *"Pass ye into me,"* saith God, *"all ye who earnestly seek after me."* But how is it we pass into God? We leave and forsake ourselves, that we may be lost in Him; and this can be effected only by annihilation; which being the true prayer of adoration, renders unto God alone, all *"Blessing, honour, glory and power, for ever and ever"* (Revelation 5:13).

This is the prayer of truth; *"It is worshipping God in spirit and in truth"* (John 4:23). "In spirit," because we enter into the purity of that Spirit which prayeth within us, and are drawn forth and freed from our own carnal and corrupt manner of praying; "In truth" because we are thereby placed in the great Truth of the All of God, and the nothing of the creature.

There are but these two truths, the All, and the nothing; everything else is falsehood. We can pay due honour to the All of God only in our own annihilation, which is no sooner accomplished, than He, who never suffers a void in nature, instantly fills us with Himself.

Did we but know the virtue and the blessings which the soul derives from this prayer, we should willingly be employed therein without ceasing. *"It is the pearl of great price: it is the hidden treasure"* (Matthew 13:44,45), which, whoever findeth, selleth freely all that he hath to purchase it: *"It is the well of living water, which springeth up unto everlasting life":* it is the adoration of God *"in spirit and in truth"* (John 4:14-23), and it is the full performance of the purest evangelical precepts.

Jesus Christ assureth us, that the *"Kingdom of God is within us"* (Luke 17:21), and this is true in two senses: First, when God becometh so fully the Master and Lord in us, that nothing resisteth His dominion; then is our interior His kingdom: And again, when we possess God, who is the Supreme Good, we possess His kingdom also, wherein there is fullness of joy, and where we attain the end of our creation: thus it is said, *"to serve God, is to reign."* The end of our creation, indeed, is to enjoy our God, even in this life; but alas! How few there are who think of this seriously.

XXI

The Noble Results
of this Species of Prayer

SOME PERSONS, WHEN THEY HEAR of the prayer of silence, falsely imagine, that the soul remains stupid, dead, and inactive. But, unquestionably, it acteth therein, more nobly and more extensively than it had ever done before; for God Himself is the mover, and the soul now acteth by the agency of His Spirit.

When St. Paul speaks of our being led by the Spirit of God, it is not meant that we should cease from action; but that we should act through the internal agency of His Grace. This is finely represented by the Prophet Ezekiel's vision of the *"wheels, which had a Living Spirit; and whithersoever the Spirit was to go, they went; they ascended, and descended, as they were moved; for the Spirit of Life was in them, and they returned not when they went"* (Ezekiel 1:9). Thus the soul should be equally subservient to the will of that Vivifying Spirit wherewith it is informed, and scrupulously faithful to follow only as that moves. These motions now never tend to return, in reflection on the creatures or itself; but go forward, in an incessant approach towards the chief end.

This action of the soul is attended with the utmost tranquility. When it acts of itself, the act is forced and constrained; and, therefore, it can the more easily perceive and distinguish it: but when it acteth under the influence of the Spirit of Grace, its action is so free, so easy, and so natural, that it almost seems as if it did not act at all: "*He hath set me at large, he hath delivered me, because he delighted in me*" (Psalm 18:19).

When the soul is in its central tendency, or, in other words, is returned through recollection into itself; from that moment the central attraction becomes a most potent action, infinitely surpassing in its energy every other species. Nothing, indeed, can equal the swiftness of this tendency to the centre: and though an action, yet it is so noble, so peaceful, so full of tranquility, so natural and spontaneous, that it appears to the soul as if it did not act at all.

When a wheel rolls slowly we can easily distinguish its parts; but when its motion is rapid we can distinguish nothing. So the soul, which rests in God, hath an activity exceedingly noble and elevated, yet altogether peaceful: and the more peaceful it is, the swifter is its course; because it is proportionately given up to that Spirit, by which it is moved and directed.

This attracting spirit is no other than God Himself, Who, in drawing us, causes us to run unto Him. How well did the spouse understand this when she said, "*Draw me, and we will run after thee*" (Song of Songs 1:3). Draw me unto Thee, O my Divine centre, by the secret springs of my existence, and all my powers and senses shall follow the potent magnetism! This simple attraction is both an ointment to heal, and a perfume to allure: "we follow," saith she, "the fragrance of thy perfumes"; and though so powerfully magnetic it is followed by the soul freely, and without constraint; for it is equally delightful as forcible; and whilst it attracts by its potency, it charms with its sweetness. "Draw me," saith the spouse, "and we will run after Thee." She speaketh of and to herself: "draw me,"—behold the unity of the centre, which attracteth! "We will run,"—behold the correspondence and course of all the senses and powers in following that attraction!

Instead of promoting idleness, we promote the highest activity by inculcating a total dependence on the Spirit of God as our moving principle; for it is "*in him we live, and move, and have our being*" (Acts 17:28). This meek dependence on the Spirit of God is indispensably necessary to reinstate the soul in its primeval unity and simplicity, that it may thereby attain the end of its creation.

We must, therefore, forsake our multifarious activity, to re-enter the simplicity and unity of God, in Whose image we were originally formed. "*The Spirit is one and manifold*" (Wisdom 7:22), and His unity doth not preclude His multiplicity. We enter into His unity when we are united unto His Spirit, and have one and the same Spirit with Him; and we are multiplied in respect to the outward execution of His will, without any departure from our state of union: so that when we are wholly moved by the Divine Spirit, which is infinitely active, our activity must, indeed, differ widely in its energy and degree from that which is merely our own.

We must yield ourselves to the guidance of "*Wisdom, which is more moving than any motion*" (Wisdom 7:24); and by abiding in dependence on its action, our activity will be truly efficient. "*All things were made by the Word, and without him was not anything made, that was made*" (John 1:3). God originally formed us in His own likeness; and He now informeth us with the Spirit of His Word, that "*Breath of Life*" (Genesis 2:7), which was inbreathed at our creation, in the participation whereof the Image of God consisted; and this life is a life of unity, simple, pure, intimate, and always fruitful. The Devil, having broken and deformed the Divine Image in the soul, the agency of the same Word, whose Spirit was inbreathed at our creation, is absolutely necessary for its renovation; and it can only be renewed by our being passive under Him who is to renew it: but who can restore the Image of God within us in its primeval form, save He who is the Essential Image of the Father.

Our activity should, therefore, consist in endeavoring to acquire and maintain such a state as may be most susceptible of Divine impressions, most flexile to all the operations of the Eternal Word. Whilst a tablet is unsteady, the painter is unable to delineate a true copy: so every act of our own selfish and proper spirit is productive of false and erroneous lineaments; it interrupts the work, and defeats the design of this adorable Painter; we must then remain in peace and move only when He moves us. "*Jesus Christ hath the Life, in himself*" (John 5:26), and He should be the life of every living thing.

As all action is estimable only in proportion to the dignity of the efficient principle, this action is incontestably more noble than any other. Actions produced by a Divine principle are Divine; but creaturely actions, however good they appear, are only human, or at best virtuous, even when accompanied by grace. Jesus Christ saith, He hath the Life in Himself. All other beings have only a borrowed life; but the Word hath the Life in Himself, and being communicative of His nature He desireth to communicate it to man. We should, therefore, make room for the influx of this Life, which can only be done by the ejection of the Adamical life, the suppression of the activity of self. This is agreeable to the assertion of St. Paul: *"If any man be in Christ he is a new creature: old things are passed away; behold all things are become new!"* (2 Corinthians 5:17), but this state can be accomplished only by dying to ourselves and to all our own activity, that the activity of God may be substituted in its place.

Instead, therefore, of prohibiting activity, we enjoin it; but in absolute dependence on the Spirit of God, that His activity may take place of our own. This can only be effected by the concurrence of the creature; and this concurrence can only be yielded by moderating and restraining our own activity, that the activity of God may gradually gain the ascendancy, and finally absorb all that is ours as distinguishable from it.

Jesus Christ hath exemplified this in the Gospel: Martha did what was right; but because she did it in her own spirit Christ rebuked her. The spirit of man is restless and turbulent; for which reason it does little, though it would appear to do much. *"Martha,"* saith Christ, *"thou art careful and troubled about many things, but one thing is needful; and Mary hath chosen that good part which shall not be taken away from her"* (Luke 10:41,42). And what was it that Mary had chosen? Repose, tranquility, and peace. She apparently ceased to act, that the Spirit of Christ might act in her; she ceased to live, that Christ might be her life.

This shows us how necessary it is to renounce ourselves and all our own activity, to follow Jesus Christ; and we cannot follow Him without being animated with His Spirit. Now that His Spirit may gain admission in us, it is necessary that our own proper spirit should be first expelled: *"He that is joined unto the Lord,"* saith St. Paul, *"is one spirit with him"* (1 Corinthians 6:17); and David said, *"It was good for him to draw near unto the Lord, and to put his trust in him"* (Psalm 73:28). This drawing near unto God, is the beginning of Union.

Divine Union has its commencement, its progression, and its consummation. It is first an inclination and tendency towards God: when the soul is introverted in the manner before described, it gets within the influence of the central attraction, and acquires an eager desire after Union: on a nearer approach unto God, it adheres to Him; and growing stronger and stronger in its adhesion, it finally becomes one; that is, "One Spirit with Him:" and it is thus that the spirit which had wandered and strayed from God, returns again to its proper source.

Into this process, which is the Divine motion, and the Spirit of Jesus Christ, we must necessarily enter. St. Paul saith, *"If any man hath not the Spirit of Christ, he is none of his"* (Romans 8:9): therefore, to be Christ's, we must be filled with His Spirit, and to be filled with His Spirit we must be emptied of our own. The Apostle, in the same passage, proves the necessity of this Divine influence or motion: *"As many"* saith he, *"as are led by the Spirit of God, they are the sons of God"* (Romans 8:14). The Spirit of Divine filiation is then the Spirit of Divine action or motion: he, therefore, adds, *"Ye have not received the spirit of bondage again to fear; but ye have received the Spirit of Adoption, whereby we, cry, Abba, Father."*

This Spirit is no other than the Spirit of Christ, through which we participate in His filiation; *"And this Spirit beareth witness with our Spirit, that we are the children of God"* (Romans 8:16). When the soul yields itself to the influence and motions of this Blessed Spirit, it feels the testimony of its Divine filiation; and it feels also, with superadded joy, that it hath received not the Spirit of bondage, but of liberty, even the liberty of the children of God. It then finds that it acts freely and sweetly, though with vigour and infallibility.

The Spirit of Divine action is so necessary in all things, that St. Paul, in the same passage, foundeth that necessity on our ignorance with respect to what we pray for: *"The Spirit,"* saith he, *"also helpeth our infirmities: for we know not what we should pray for as we ought; but the Spirit itself maketh intercession for us, with groanings which cannot be uttered."* This is positive; if we know not what we stand in need of, nor pray, as we ought to do, for those things which are necessary; and if the Spirit which is in us, and to which we resign ourselves, asks and intercedes for us; should we not give unlimited freedom to its action, to its ineffable groanings in our behalf?

This Spirit is the Spirit of the Word which is always heard, as He saith Himself: *"I know that thou hearest me always"* (John 11:42); and if we freely admit this Spirit to pray and intercede in us, we also shall be always heard. The reason of this is given us by the same Apostle, that skillful Mystic, and Master of the Internal life, where he adds, *"He that searcheth the heart, knoweth what is the mind of the Spirit; because he maketh intercession for the saints, according to the will of God"* (Romans 8:27). That is to say, the Spirit demandeth only that which is conformable to the will of God; and the will of God is, that we should be saved: that we should become perfect: He, therefore, intercedeth for that which is necessary for so great an end.

Why should we then burden ourselves with superfluous cares, and fatigue and weary ourselves in the multiplicity of our ways, without ever saying, "Let us rest in peace?" God Himself inviteth us to cast our cares, our anxieties, upon Him; and He complains in Isaiah, with ineffable goodness, that the soul had expended its powers and its treasures on a thousand external objects, and mistook its path to happiness, which was attainable by means much more facile: *"Wherefore,"* saith God, *"do you spend money for that which is not bread? And your labour for that which satisfieth not? Hearken diligently unto me, and eat ye that which is good, and let your soul delight itself in fatness"* (Isaiah 55:2).

Did we but know the blessedness of thus hearkening unto God, and how greatly the soul is strengthened and invigorated thereby, *"All flesh would surely be silent before the Lord"* (Zechariah 2:13); all would cease and be still, as soon as He appears. But to engage us farther in a boundless resignation, God assures us, by the same Prophet, that we should fear nothing in this abandonment, because He takes a care of us, surpassing the highest tenderness of which we can form an idea: *"Can a woman"* saith He, *"forget her sucking child, that she should not have compassion on the son of her womb? Yea, she may forget; yet will I not forget thee"* (Isaiah 49:15). O blessed assurance, pregnant with consolation! Who, after this, shall be fearful of resigning themselves wholly to the dispensations and guidance of their God?

XXII

Of Internal Acts

ACTS ARE DISTINGUISHED into external and internal. External acts are those which bear relation to some sensible object, and are either morally good or evil, merely according to the nature of the principle from which they proceed. I intend here to speak only of Internal acts, those energies of the soul, by which it turns internally to some objects, and averts from others.

If during my application to God I should form a will to change the nature of my act, I thereby withdraw myself from God, and turn to created objects, and that in a greater or less degree according to the strength of the act: and if, when I am turned towards the creature, I would return to God, I must necessarily form an act for that purpose; and the more perfect this act is, the more complete is the conversion.

Till conversion is perfected, many reiterated acts are necessary; for it is generally progressive, though with some it is almost instantaneous. My act, however, should consist in a continual turning unto God, an exertion of every faculty and power of the soul purely for Him, agreeably to the instructions of the Son of Sirach: *"Re-unite all the motions of thy heart in the holiness of God"* and to the example of David, *"I will keep my whole strength for thee"* (Psalm 58:10), which is done by earnestly re-entering into one's self. As Isaiah saith, *"Return to your heart"* (Isaiah 46:8); for we have strayed from our heart by sin, and it is our heart only that God requires, *"My son give me thine heart, and let thine eye observe my ways"* (Proverbs 23:26). To give the heart to God is to have the whole eternal energy of the soul ever centering in Him, that we may be rendered conformable to His will. We must, therefore, continue invariably turned to God from our very first application to Him.

But the soul being weak and unstable, and accustomed to turn to external objects, is consequently prone to dissipation. This evil, however, will be counteracted if the soul, on perceiving the aberration, by a pure act of return to God, instantly replaces itself again in Him; and this act subsists as long as the conversion by the powerful influence of a simple and unfeigned return to God lasts: and as many reiterated acts form a habit, the soul contracts the habit of conversion, and that act which was before interrupted and distinct becomes continual.

The soul should not then be perplexed about forming an act which already subsists, and which, indeed, it cannot attempt to form without difficulty and constraint; it even finds that it is withdrawn from its proper state under pretense of seeking that which is in reality acquired, seeing the habit is already formed and is confirmed in habitual conversion and habitual love. It is seeking one act by the help of many, instead of continuing attached to God by one simple act alone.

We may remark that at times we form with facility many distinct yet simple acts, which shows that we have wandered, and that we re-enter our heart after having strayed from it; yet when we have re-entered we should remain there in peace. We err, therefore, in supposing that we do not form acts; we form them continually, but they should be in their nature conformable to the degree of our spiritual advancement.

The greatest difficulty with most spiritual people arises from their not clearly comprehending this matter. Now some acts are transient and distinct, others are continual; and again, some are direct, and others reflex. All cannot form the first, neither are all in a state suited to form the last. The first are adapted to those who have strayed, and who require a distinguishable exertion, proportioned to the degree of their deviation, which, if inconsiderable, an act of the most simple kind is sufficient.

By the continued act I mean that whereby the soul is altogether turned toward God in a direct tendency, which always subsists, and which it doth not renew unless it has been interrupted. The soul being thus turned is in charity, and abides therein, *"and he that dwelleth in love dwelleth in God"* (1 John 4:16). The soul then, as it were, existeth and reposeth in this habitual act, but free from sloth or torpor; for still there is an unintermitted act subsisting, which is a sweet sinking into the Deity, whose attraction becomes more and more powerful; and in following this potent attraction, the soul presses farther, and sinks continually deeper, into the ocean of Divine love, maintaining an activity infinitely more powerful, vigorous, and effectual than that which served to accomplish its first return.

Now the soul that is thus profoundly and vigorously active, being wholly given up to God, doth not perceive its activity, because it is direct and not reflex; and this is the cause why some, who do not express themselves properly, say that they do not act at all; but it is a mistake, for they were never more truly or nobly active: they should rather say that they did not distinguish their acts than that they did not act. I allow they do not act of themselves, but they are drawn, and they follow the attraction. Love is the weight which sinks them into God, as into an infinite sea, wherein they descend with inconceivable rapidity from one profound depth to another.

It is then an impropriety to say that we do not form acts: all form acts, but the manner of their formation is not alike in all. The cause of the mistake is this, all who know they should act are desirous of acting distinguishably and perceptibly. But this cannot be; distinct and sensible acts are for beginners, and acts of a higher nature for those in a more advanced state. To stop in the former, which are weak and of little profit, is to debar one's self of the latter; and again, to attempt the latter without having passed through the former is a no less considerable error.

All things should then be done in their season. Every state has its commencement, its progress, and its consummation; and it is an unhappy error to stop in the beginning. There is even no art but what hath its progress; and at first we must labour with diligence and toil, but at last we shall reap the harvest of our industry. When the vessel is in port the mariners are obliged to exert all their strength that they may clear her thence and put to sea; but at length they turn her with facility as they please. In like manner, while the soul remains in sin and creaturely entanglements, very frequent and strenuous endeavours are requisite to effect its freedom; the cords which withhold it must be loosed; and then by strong and vigorous efforts it gathers itself inwards, pushing off gradually from the old port; and in leaving that at a distance it proceeds to the interior, the haven to which it wishes to steer.

When the vessel is thus turned, in proportion as she advances on the sea, she leaves the land behind; and the farther she departs from the old harbour, the less difficulty and labour is requisite in moving her forward: at length she begins to get sweetly under sail and now proceeds so swiftly in her course that the oars which have become useless are laid aside. How is the pilot now employed? He is content with spreading the sails and holding the rudder. To spread the sails is to lay one's self before God in the prayer of simple exposition, that we may be acted upon by His Spirit: to hold the rudder is to restrain our hearts from wandering from the true course, recalling it gently, and guiding it steadily to the dictates of the Blessed Spirit, which gradually gain possession and dominion of the heart, just as the wind by degrees fills the sails and impels the vessel. While the winds are fair the pilot and mariners rest from their labours, and the vessel glides rapidly along without their toil; and when they thus repose and leave the vessel to the wind, they make more way in one hour than they had done in a length of time by all their former efforts: were they even now to attempt using the oar they would not only fatigue themselves, but retard the vessel by their ill-timed labours.

This is the manner of acting we should pursue interiorly; it will, indeed, advance us in a short time, by the Divine impulsion, infinitely farther than a whole life spent in reiterated acts of self-exertion; and whosoever will take this path will find it easier than any other.

If the wind is contrary and blows a storm, we must cast anchor to withhold the vessel: our anchor is a firm confidence and hope in our God, waiting patiently the calming of the tempest and the return of a favourable gale as David *waited patiently for the Lord, and He inclined unto him and heard his cry* (Psalm 40:1). We must, therefore, be resigned to the Spirit of God, giving up ourselves wholly to His Divine Guidance.

XXIII

To Pastors and Teachers

IF ALL WHO LABOURED for the conversion of others were to introduce them immediately into prayer and the Interior Life, and make it their main design to gain and win over the heart, numberless as well as permanent conversions would certainly ensue. On the contrary, few and transient fruits must attend that labour which is confined to outward matters; such as burdening the disciple with a thousand precepts for external exercises, instead of leaving the soul to Christ by the occupation of the heart in Him.

If ministers were solicitous thus to instruct their parishioners; shepherds, while they watched their flocks, might have the Spirit of the primitive Christians, and the husbandman at the plough maintain a blessed intercourse with his God; the manufacturer, while he exhausts his outward man with labour, would be renewed in internal strength; and every species of vice would shortly disappear and every parishioner become a true follower of the Good Shepherd.

O when once the heart is gained, how easily is all moral evil corrected! it is, therefore, that God, above all things, requires the heart. It is the conquest of the heart alone that can extirpate those dreadful vices which are so predominant, such as drunkenness, blasphemy, lewdness, envy, and theft. Jesus Christ would become the universal and peaceful Sovereign, and the face of the Church would be wholly renewed.

The decay of internal piety is unquestionably the source of the various errors that have arisen in the Church; all which would speedily be sapped and overthrown should inward religion be re-established. Errors are only so far prejudicial to the soul as they tend to weaken faith and deter from prayer; and if, instead of engaging our wandering brethren in vain disputes, we could but teach them simply to believe and diligently to pray, we should lead them sweetly unto God.

O how inexpressibly great is the loss sustained by mankind from the neglect of the Interior Life! And how tremendous must the great day of retribution be to those who are entrusted with the care of souls, for not having discovered and dispensed to their flock this hidden treasure.

Some excuse themselves by saying that this is a dangerous way; pleading the incapacity of simple persons to comprehend spiritual matters. But the Oracles of Truth affirm the contrary: "*The Lord loveth those who walk simply*" (Proverbs 12:22). And where can be the danger of walking in the only true way, which is Jesus Christ? Of giving up ourselves to Him, fixing our eye continually upon Him, placing all our confidence in His grace, and tending with all the strength of our soul to His pure Love?

The simple ones, so far from being incapable of this perfection, are, by their docility, innocence, and humility, peculiarly adapted and qualified for its attainment; and as they are not accustomed to reasoning, they are less employed in speculations, less tenacious of their own opinions. Even from their want of learning, they submit more freely to the teachings of the Divine Spirit; whereas others, who are blinded by self-sufficiency and enslaved by prejudice, give great resistance to the operations of grace.

We are told in Scripture "*that unto the simple God giveth the understanding of his law*" (Psalm 119:130); and we are also assured that God loveth to commune freely with them: "*The Lord careth for the simple; I was reduced to extremity,*

105

and he saved me" (Psalm 114:6). To warn Spiritual Fathers against preventing the little ones from coming to Christ, He Himself said to His Apostles, "*Suffer little children to come unto me, for of such is the kingdom of Heaven*" (Matthew 19:14). It was the endeavor of the Apostles to prevent children from going to our Lord, which occasioned this gracious charge. Man frequently applies a remedy to the outward body, whilst the disease lies at the heart.

The cause of our being so unsuccessful in reforming mankind, especially those of the lower class, is our beginning with external matters; all our labours in this field do but produce such fruit as endures not: but if the key of the interior be first given, the exterior would be naturally and easily reformed. To teach man to seek God in his heart, to think of Him, to return to Him whenever he finds that he has wandered from Him, and to do and to suffer all things with a single eye to please Him, is the natural and ready process; it is leading the soul to the very source of grace, wherein is to be found all that is necessary for sanctification.

I, therefore, conjure you all, O ye who have the care of souls, to put them at once into this way, which is Jesus Christ; nay, it is He Himself who conjures you, by the precious Blood He hath shed for those entrusted to you, "*to speak to the heart of Jerusalem*" (Isaiah 40:2). O ye

Dispensers of His Grace, ye Preachers of His Word, ye Ministers of His Sacraments, establish His Kingdom!—and that it may indeed be established, make Him Ruler over the hearts of His subjects! For as it is the heart alone that can oppose His Sovereignty, it is by the subjection of the heart that His Sovereignty is most highly exalted: "*Give glory to the holiness of God, and he shall become your sanctification*" (Isaiah 8:13). Compose catechisms particularly to teach prayer, not by reasoning nor by method, for the simple are incapable thereof; but to teach the prayer of the heart, not of the understanding; the prayer of God's Spirit, not of man's invention.

Alas! by wanting them to pray in elaborate forms, and to be curiously critical therein, you create their chief obstacles. The children have been led astray from the best of Fathers, by your endeavouring to teach them too refined, too polished a language. Go then, ye poor children, to your Heavenly Father; speak to Him in your natural language; and though it be ever so rude and barbarous in the opinion of men, it is not so to Him. A Father is much better pleased with an address which love and respect in the child throws into disorder, because He knows it proceeds from the heart, than by a formal and barren harangue, though ever so elaborate in the composition.

The simple and undisguised emotions of filial love are infinitely more expressive than all language and all reasoning.

By forming instructions about how to love by rule and method the Essential Love, men have in a great measure estranged themselves from Him. O how unnecessary is it to teach an art of loving! The language of love, though natural to the lover, is nonsense and barbarism to him who loveth not. The best way to learn the love of God is to love Him. The ignorant and simple, because they proceed with more cordiality and simplicity, often become most perfect therein. The Spirit of God needs none of our arrangements and methods; when it pleaseth Him, He turns shepherds into prophets: and, so far from excluding any from the Temple of Prayer, He throws wide the gates, that all may enter; while Wisdom cries aloud in the highways, *"Whoso is simple let him turn in hither"* (Proverbs 9:4); and to the fools she saith, *"Come eat of my bread, and drink of the wine which I have mingled"* (Proverbs 9:5). And doth not Jesus Christ Himself thank His Father for having *"hid the secrets of his kingdom from the wise and prudent and revealed them unto babes?"* (Matthew 11:25).

XXIV

Of the way to Attain Divine Union

IT IS IMPOSSIBLE TO ATTAIN Divine Union solely by the activity of meditation, or by the melting of the affections, or even by the highest degree of luminous and distinctly comprehended prayer. There are many reasons for this, the chief of which are as follow:—

First, according to Scripture, "*no man shall see God and live*" (Exodus 33:20). Now all the exercises of discursive prayer, and even of active contemplation, while esteemed as the summit and end of the passive, and not merely as a preparative to it, are still living exercises by which we cannot see God; that is to say, be united with Him; for all that is of man's own power or exertion must first die, be it ever so noble, ever so exalted.

St. John relates "*That there was a great silence in heaven*" (Revelation 8:1). Now heaven represents the foundation and centre of the soul, wherein, ere the Majesty of God appears, all must be hushed to silence. All the efforts, nay, the very existence of self-sufficiency must be destroyed, because nothing is opposite to God but self-sufficiency; and all the malignity of man is in this failing, as in the power of its evil nature, insomuch that the purity of a soul increases in proportion as it loses this quality; till at length that which had been a fault, while the soul lived in self-sufficiency and so acted, becomes no longer such, from the purity and innocence it hath acquired by departing from that which caused the dissimilitude between it and God.

Secondly, to unite two things so opposite as the impurity of the creature and the purity of God, the simplicity of God and the multiplicity of man, much more is requisite than the impotent efforts of the creature: no less than a singular and efficacious operation of the Almighty can ever accomplish this, for things must be reduced to some familiarity before they can blend and become one. Can the impurity of dross be united with the purity of gold? What then does God do? He sends His own Wisdom before Him, as the last fire shall be sent upon earth to destroy by its activity all that is impure therein; and as nothing can resist the power of that fire, in like manner this Wisdom dissolves and destroys all the impurities of the creature and disposes it for Divine Union.

This impurity, so opposite to Union, consists in self-sufficiency and activity.

This is the source and fountain of all that defilement and corruption which can never be allied to Essential Purity; the rays of the sun may glance, indeed, upon filth and mire, but can never be united with them. Activity obstructs Union; for God being an infinite stillness, the soul, in order to be united to Him, must participate in this stillness, else the contrariety between stillness and activity would prevent assimilation.

Therefore, the soul can never arrive at Divine Union but by the repose or stillness of the will, nor can it ever become One with God but by being re-established in the purity of its first creation, that is, in this central repose.

God purifies the soul by His Wisdom, as refiners do metals in the furnace. Gold cannot be purified but by fire, which gradually separates from and consumes all that is earthy and heterogeneous: it must be melted and dissolved, and all impure mixtures taken away by casting it again and again into the furnace; thus it is refined from all internal corruption, and even exalted to a state incapable of farther purification.

The goldsmith now no longer discovers any adulterate mixture; its purity is perfect, its simplicity complete. The fire no longer touches it; and were it to remain an age in the furnace its purity would not be increased nor its substance diminished. Then is it fit for the most exquisite workmanship: and if thereafter this gold seems obscured or defiled, it is no more than an accidental defilement contracted by its contiguity to some impure body; but this is only superficial, and widely different from its former impurity, which was hidden in the very centre and ground of its nature and, as it were, identified with it. Those, however, who are ignorant of this process and its blessed effects would be apt to despise and reject the vessel of pure gold sullied by some external pollution, and prefer an impure and gross metal that appeared superficially bright and polished.

Farther, the goldsmith never mingles together the pure and the impure gold, lest the dross of the one should corrupt the other; before they can be united they must first be equally refined; he therefore plunges the impure metal into the furnace till all its dross is purged away and it becomes fully prepared for incorporation and union with the pure gold.

This is what St. Paul means when he declares that *"the fire shall try every man's work of what sort it is"* (1 Corinthians 3:13). He adds, *"If any man's work be burnt, he shall suffer loss; yet he himself shall be saved, yet so as by fire*" (1 Corinthians 3:15). He here intimates that there is a species of works so degraded by impure mixtures that though the mercy of God accepts them, yet they must pass through the fire to be purged from the contamination of Self; and it is in this sense that God is said to "*examine and judge our righteousness*" (Psalm 14:3), because that, "*by the deeds of the law, there shall no flesh be justified, but by the righteousness of God, which is by faith in Jesus Christ*" (Romans 3:20).

Thus we see that the Divine justice and wisdom, as an unremitting fire, must devour and destroy all that is earthly, sensual, and carnal, and all self-activity, before the soul can be fitted for and capable of Union with God. Now this purification can never be accomplished by the industry of fallen man; on the contrary, he submits to it always with reluctance: he is so enamoured of self, and so averse to its destruction, that did not God act upon him powerfully and with authority, he would forever resist.

It may, perhaps, be objected here that as God never robs man of his free will, he can always resist the Divine operations, and that I therefore err in saying God acts thus absolutely and without the consent of man.

Let me, however, explain myself. By man's giving a passive consent, God, without usurpation, may assume full power and entire guidance; for having, in the beginning of his conversion, made an unreserved surrender of himself to all that God wills of him or by him, he thereby gave an active consent to whatsoever God thereafter might operate or require. But when God begins to burn, destroy, and purify, then the soul, not perceiving the salutary design of these operations, shrinks from them: and as the gold seems rather to blacken than brighten when first put into the furnace, so it conceives that its purity is lost and that its temptations are sins; insomuch that if an active and explicit consent were then requisite the soul could scarcely give it, nay, often would withhold it. The utmost the soul can do is to remain firm in a passive disposition, enduring as well as it is able all these Divine operations, which it neither can nor will obstruct.

In this manner, therefore, the soul is purified from all proper, distinct, perceptible, and multiplied operations which constitute the great dissimilitude between it and God: it is rendered, by degrees, conformed, and then uniform; and the passive capacity of the creature is elevated, ennobled, and enlarged, though in a secret and hidden manner, and therefore called mystical: but in all these operations the soul must concur passively. It is true, indeed, that at the beginning of its purification activity is requisite; which as the Divine operations become stronger and stronger it must gradually cease, yielding itself up to the impulses of the Divine Spirit, till wholly absorbed in Him. But this is often a difficult and tedious process.

We do not then say, as some have falsely supposed, that there is no need of action in the process of Divine purification; on the contrary, we affirm it is the gate; at which, however, we would not have those stop who are to obtain ultimate perfection, which is impractible, except the first helps are laid aside: for, however necessary they may have been at the entrance of the road, they become afterwards mere clogs, and greatly detrimental to those who adhere to them, preventing them from ever arriving at the end of their course. This made St. Paul say, *"Forgetting those things which are behind and reaching forth to those which are before, I press toward the mark for the prize of the high calling in Christ Jesus"* (Philippians 3:13).

Would you not say that he had lost his senses, who, having undertaken an important journey, should fix his abode at the first inn because he had been told that many travelers who had come that way had lodged in the house and made it their place of residence? All that we would wish then is, that souls should press toward the mark, should pursue their journey, and take the shortest and easiest road; not stopping at the first stage, but following the counsel and example of St. Paul, suffer themselves to be guided and governed by the Spirit of Grace which would infallibly conduct them to the end of their creation, the enjoyment of God. But while we confess that the enjoyment of God is the end for which alone we were created; that without holiness none can attain it: and that to attain it, we must necessarily pass through a severe and purifying process; how strange is it that we should dread and avoid this process, as if that could be the cause of evil or imperfection in the present life, which is to be productive of glory and blessedness in the life to come!

None can be ignorant that God is the Supreme Good; that essential blessedness consists in Union with Him; that the saints are more or less glorified, according as this Union is more or less advanced; and that the soul cannot attain this Union by the mere activity of its own powers: for God communicates Himself to the soul in proportion as its passive capacity is great, noble, and extensive; it cannot be united to God but in simplicity and passivity; and as this Union is beatitude itself, the way to it in simplicity and passivity, instead of being evil, must be good, must be most free from delusion and danger, the safest, the surest, and the best.

Would Jesus Christ have made this the most perfect and necessary way had there been evil or danger therein? No! all can travel this road to blessedness; and all are called thereto, as to the enjoyment of God, which alone is beatitude, both in this world and the next. I say the enjoyment of God Himself and not His gifts which, as they do not constitute essential beatitude, cannot fully content an immortal spirit: the soul is so noble, so great, that the most exalted gifts of God cannot fill its immense capacity with happiness unless the Giver also bestows Himself. Now the whole desire of the Divine Being is to give Himself to every creature, according to the capacity with which it is endued; and yet, alas! how reluctantly man suffers himself to be drawn to God! how fearful is he to prepare for Divine Union!

Some say that we should not attempt, by our own ability, to place ourselves in this state. I grant it: but what a poor subterfuge is this? Since I have all along asserted and proved that the utmost exertion of the highest created being could never accomplish this of itself: it is God alone must do it. The creature may, indeed, open the window; but it is the sun himself that must give the light.

The same persons say again that some may feign to have attained this blessed state: but, alas! none can any more feign this than the wretch, who is on the point of perishing with hunger can for a length of time feign to be full and satisfied; some wish or word, some sigh or sign, will inevitably escape him, and betray his famished state.

Since then none can attain this blessed state save those whom God Himself leads and places therein, we do not pretend to introduce any into it, but only to point out the shortest and safest road that leads to it: beseeching you not to be retarded in your progress by any external exercises, not to sit down a resident at the first inn, nor to be satisfied with the sweets which are tasted in the milk for babes. If the water of eternal life is shown to some thirsty souls, how inexpressibly cruel would it be, by confining them to a round of external forms, to prevent their approaching it, so that their longing shall never be satisfied but they shall perish with thirst!

Let us all agree in the way, as we all agree in the end, which is evident and incontrovertible. The way has its beginning, progress, and end; and the nearer we approach the end, the farther is the beginning behind us; it is only by proceeding from one that we can ever arrive at the other. Would you get from the entrance to the distant end of the road without passing over the intermediate space? And surely, if the end is good, holy, and necessary, and the entrance also good, can that be condemnable, as evil, which is the necessary passage, the direct road leading from the one to the other?

O ye blind and foolish men, who pride yourselves on science, wisdom, wit, and power, how well do you verify what God hath said, that *"His Secrets are hidden from the great and wise, and revealed unto the little ones—the babes!"*

Notes

Jeanne Guyon

Jeanne-Marie Bouvier de la Motte-Guyon, more commonly known as Madame Guyon, was an aristocrat by birth, a widow and mother to three, and cousin to the famous François Fénelon. Her early religious training and later mystical experiences led her to passionately live and teach a message of direct access to the Presence of God. These notions were an offense to the political and religious authorities of her day. She was imprisoned in the Bastille from 1695 to 1703 by king Louis XIV after publishing the book, A Short and Very Easy Method of Prayer (re-published here as The Simple Way of Prayer). Her work endures to this day, calling everyday Christians beyond mere religious ritual into a personal experience with the Living Spirit of Jesus.

ABOUT

SEA HARP TIMELESS

The Sea Harp Timeless series, by Sea Harp Press, is a collection of the greatest writings ever composed about Jesus of Nazareth, His Kingdom, His Holy Spirit, the Father of Heaven, the Early Church, the Christian life, one's inner life, and what it means to "abide." The men and women whose works we choose to comprise this series are those whose voices still rise above the march of time; whose words endure with a power only attributable to the workings of the Holy Spirit.

Our hope is that, by re-awakening the Body of Christ's interest in such "Christian classics," we may help the Church of today return to its simpler, more primitive roots. For, indeed, if a single thread is detectible across the centuries spanned by our Timeless series, it would run like this:

"We must all encounter Jesus, alive, every single day."

We pray that this offering, and the other works in this collection, will lead your heart to fresh, direct experience of Him; that the "best of the past" will find their home in you. May we ever seek to know Him better!

A B O U T
SEA HARP PRESS

Sea Harp is a specialty press with one overarching aim: in the words of Andrew Murray, to "be much occupied with Jesus, and believe much in Him, as the True Vine." Our mission is twofold: to reinvigorate the Church's reading of the best of the past, and to bring out fresh editions of both today's and tomorrow's classics — all for the purpose of personal encounter with Jesus Himself.

For every piece of media we consider publishing, we ask two fundamental questions:

- Is this work entirely about the person of Jesus of Nazareth?
- Would the Early Church have thought this work worthy of sharing?

We take our name from the original Hebrew word for the Sea of Galilee—*Kinneret*: כִּנֶּרֶת: meaning "harp"—which was given because of the harp-like shape of the shoreline around which Jesus ministered. It was, in less words, a place known as the Harp-Sea.

Thank you for joining us as we walk the Way with that most wonderful Man of Galilee.

the
SEA *of*
GALILEE

W W W . S E A H A R P . C O M

Made in United States
Orlando, FL
20 September 2022

22612367R00079